WHAT ARE SEA INVERTEBRATES?

JULIA J. QUINLAN

Britannica®
Educational Publishing

IN ASSOCIATION WITH

ROSEN
EDUCATIONAL SERVICES

Published in 2017 by Britannica Educational Publishing (a trademark of Encyclopædia Britannica, Inc.) in association with The Rosen Publishing Group, Inc.
29 East 21st Street, New York, NY 10010

Distributed exclusively by Rosen Publishing.
To see additional Britannica Educational Publishing titles, go to rosenpublishing.com.

First Edition

Britannica Educational Publishing
J.E. Luebering: Executive Director, Core Editorial
Mary Rose McCudden: Editor, Britannica Student Encyclopedia

Rosen Publishing
Jacob R. Steinberg: Editor
Nelson Sá: Art Director
Brian Garvey: Designer
Cindy Reiman: Photography Manager
Karen Huang: Photo Researcher

Library of Congress Cataloging-in-Publication Data

Names: Quinlan, Julia J., author.
Title: What are sea invertebrates? / Julia J. Quinlan.
Description: First edition. | New York, NY : Britannica Educational
  Publishing in association with Rosen Educational Services, 2017. | Series:
  Let's find out! Marine life | Includes bibliographical references and
  index.
Identifiers: LCCN 2016029697 | ISBN 9781508103899 (library bound) |
  ISBN 9781508103905 (pbk.) | ISBN 9781508103165 (6-pack)
Subjects: LCSH: Marine invertebrates—Juvenile literature.
Classification: LCC QL365.363 .Q46 2016 | DDC 592.177—dc23

Manufactured in China

Photo credits: Cover, p. 1, interior pages background image Christopher Gardiner/Shutterstock.com; pp. 4, 28 Encyclopædia Britannica, Inc.; p. 5 Mana Photo/Shutterstock.com; p. 6 Alexander Rieber/EyeEm/Getty Images; p. 7 Kondratuk A/Shutterstock.com; p. 8 Dario Sabljak/Shutterstock.com; 9 © Richard Carey/Fotolia; p. 10 prochasson frederic/Shutterstock.com; p. 11 maikbrand/Shutterstock.com; p. 12 Richard A. McMillin/Shutterstock.com; pp. 12–13 Christian Darkin/Science Source; pp. 14–15 © Digital Vision/Getty Images; p. 15 © Corbis; pp. 16–17 Heinrich van den Berg/Gallo Images/Getty Images; p. 17 Sharon Eisenzopf/Shutterstock.com; p. 18 © Comstock/Thinkstock; pp. 18–19 Bodil Bluhm and Katrin Iken—NOAA/Census of Marine Life; p. 20 NatureDiver/Shutterstock.com; p. 21 Ingrid Maasik/Shutterstock.com; p. 22 Dennis Sabo/Shutterstock.com; p. 23 Danita Delimont/Gallo Images/Getty Images; p. 24 KGrif/iStock/Thinkstock; p. 25 Alex Robinson/AWL Images/Getty Images; p. 26 Neil Overy/Gallo Images/Getty Images; pp. 26–27 Danté Fenolio/Science Source; pp. 28–29 Roberta Olenick/All Canada Photos/Getty Images.

CONTENTS

What Is a Sea Invertebrate?

An invertebrate is an animal without a backbone. An animal with a backbone is called a vertebrate. Humans, dogs, and whales are examples of vertebrates. Worms, bees, and snails are examples of invertebrates. Invertebrates live in every part of the world. In fact, most of the animals on Earth are invertebrates. Invertebrates come in all different shapes and sizes.

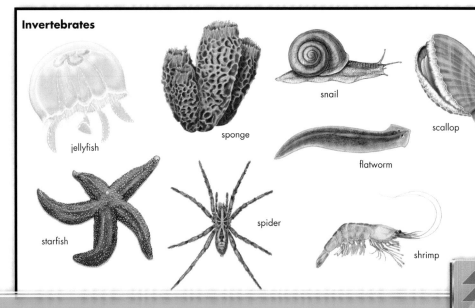

Invertebrates

jellyfish

sponge

snail

scallop

flatworm

starfish

spider

shrimp

Sponges, flatworms, jellyfish, sea stars, spiders, shrimp, snails, and scallops are just a few of the many kinds of invertebrates.

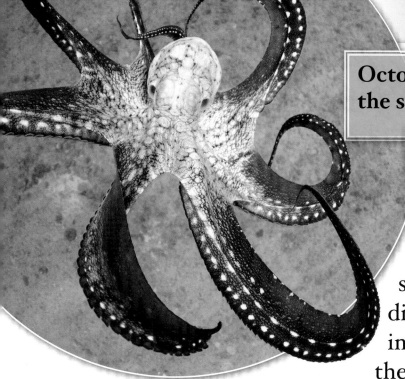

Octopuses are known as one of the smartest invertebrates.

A sea invertebrate is an invertebrate that lives in the sea. There are many different groups of invertebrates that live in the world's oceans. These animals have such features as stinging tentacles, spiny skin, soft bodies, or an exoskeleton. Some, like sponges, are very simple. Sponges are merely a mass of specialized cells. Others, like octopuses, are more complex. Octopuses can change skin color very quickly and have been observed using tools.

COMPARE AND CONTRAST

Based on what you know about vertebrates and invertebrates, think of ways that both types of animals are similar. In what ways are they different?

OCTOPUSES

Octopuses belong to a group of invertebrates called mollusks. Other mollusks include squid, clams, and oysters. There are more than 150 species of octopus, and they live in seas throughout the world. Octopuses are considered the smartest invertebrates.

Octopuses have eight arms and soft, baglike bodies with large eyes. Their long, slender arms reach out in all

Here you can see the rows of suckers on the underside of an octopus's arm.

THINK ABOUT IT

Octopuses have eight arms. Can you think of another animal that has eight arms or legs?

The giant Pacific octopus is the largest and longest-living octopus species. The largest ever found weighed 600 pounds (272 kilograms).

directions. Each arm has two rows of cuplike suckers with great holding power.

Octopuses vary greatly in size. The smallest are only about 2 inches (5 centimeters) long. The largest may be 18 feet (5.5 meters) long and have a 30-foot (9-meter) arm span.

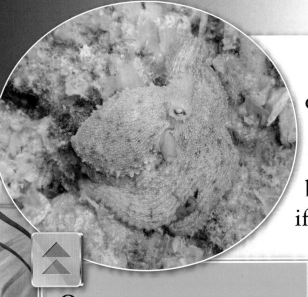

Octopuses can change color quickly depending on their surroundings or their mood. They can be gray, brown, pink, blue, green, or even an angry red if they are suddenly frightened.

An octopus usually crawls along the ocean bottom searching for food. It eats mainly crabs and lobsters. Octopuses are skillful hunters. They can attack large prey, such as sharks. If an octopus is in danger, it shoots a jet of water out of its body. This moves the octopus backward very quickly. Octopuses can also release a cloud of ink to confuse an enemy. The ink can also affect the attacker's senses. This makes it hard for the predator to track them. Octopuses' soft bodies

Octopuses are masters of disguise. They blend into their surroundings to stay safe and to sneak up on prey.

VOCABULARY

A **predator** is an animal that lives by killing and eating other animals.

The day octopus lives in tropical waters with a range from Hawaii to East Africa. Unlike most octopuses, day octopuses hunt during the day!

allow them to squeeze into extremely small places where predators can't reach them.

A female octopus lays her eggs under rocks or in holes. She guards the eggs for four to eight weeks. Upon hatching, the young drift for several weeks before going to the ocean bottom.

JELLYFISH

Jellyfish are another kind of invertebrate. They have soft, jellylike bodies and no bones. Jellyfish are members of a group of animals called cnidarians. There are about 200 species of jellyfish. They are found in all oceans. Most live near the surface of the water. Jellyfish

VOCABULARY

Cnidarians are a group of animals that includes jellyfish, corals, and sea anemones. All cnidarians produce stinging capsules.

Jellyfish often just drift on ocean currents, though some can move by creating changes in those currents.

10

have existed for hundreds of millions of years—since even before dinosaurs roamed the planet!

A typical jellyfish is shaped like an unfolded umbrella. Some jellyfish are barely big enough to be seen. Others are more than 6 feet (2 meters) across. The largest jellyfish species is the lion's mane jellyfish. Its tentacles can be up to 120 feet (36.5 meters) long.

Lion's mane jellyfish live in the cold waters of the Arctic, northern Atlantic, and northern Pacific oceans.

Jellyfish can be transparent, white, brown, pink, blue, or maroon. Certain jellyfish are luminescent, meaning they glow. Some jellyfish have eyes around the edge of the body. The mouth and

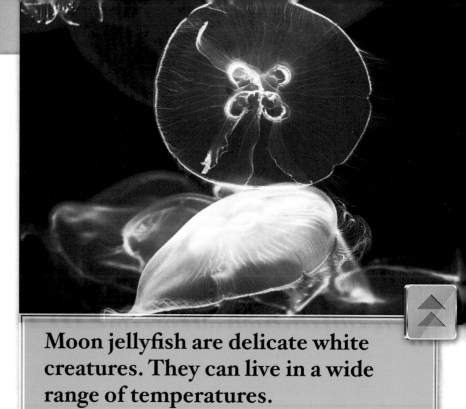

Moon jellyfish are delicate white creatures. They can live in a wide range of temperatures.

stomach are in the middle of the body. Jellyfish swim by contracting muscles on the underside of the body.

A jellyfish may have a few or many tentacles. Thin tentacles run around the edge of the body. Four or more larger tentacles hang down from the middle of the body, below the mouth. The tentacles are lined with stinging cells that make poison. The poison can

COMPARE AND CONTRAST

What do jellyfish and octopuses have in common? How are they different?

stun small animals. The tentacles then pull the animals into the mouth. Most jellyfish eat tiny animals known as plankton.

Certain jellyfish can be very dangerous to humans. Even a small sting from the jellyfish called sea wasps can kill a person within a few minutes. Jellyfish do not attack humans on purpose, though. Most stings occur when a person accidentally touches a jellyfish.

A sea wasp's sting can be deadly to humans, but some other creatures are immune to the sting.

CORALS

Corals live in every ocean. Some live in enormous colonies called reefs. The largest is the Great Barrier Reef off the coast of Australia. Coral reefs are home to many other plants and animals in addition to the coral itself.

The body of a coral is called a polyp. The polyp attaches to a surface. Polyps can be .04 inch (1 millimeter) to 10 inches (25 centimeters) across. At the top of the polyp is the mouth. The mouth is surrounded by

Coral comes in many different colors. Many fish live in and around coral because it provides protection.

tentacles that paralyze prey and bring the prey into the mouth.

Corals have a skeleton that may be outside or inside the body. Stony corals have a hard, outside skeleton made of a mineral called calcium carbonate.

Corals produce eggs that develop into tiny creatures called planulae. Planulae develop into polyps. Corals also reproduce by budding. A bud is a new polyp that develops on the body of an old polyp. Some types of coral may live for hundreds of years.

THINK ABOUT IT
Coral reefs are often called "rainforests of the sea." Why do you think that is?

This coral's tentacles are spreading out in search of food. At the center is the coral's mouth.

SEA ANEMONES

Sea anemones look like flowers but are actually animals. Their "petals" are their tentacles. Like jellyfish and corals, sea anemones use their tentacles to catch their food. They eat shrimp, fish, and other small animals. Their tentacles may be red, yellow, green, blue, orange, brown, white, or a mix of colors. There are more than 1,000 species of sea anemone.

Sea anemones have soft bodies that may be thick and short or long and slender. Most of the body is made up of water. Sea anemones range from less than an inch (2.5

THINK ABOUT IT

One kind of hermit crab often carries one or more sea anemones on its back. Can you think of how this might help the hermit crab?

centimeters) to about 5 feet (1.5 meters) across.

Some sea anemones live together in groups, like these anemones that live off the coast of Oregon.

Most sea anemones rarely move. Some glide slowly or do slow somersaults. Sea anemones are usually attached to a hard surface like a rock, a seashell, or the back of a crab. Some sea anemones float near the ocean's surface or burrow into sand or mud.

Sea anemones can be found in oceans all around the world. This anemone lives in the waters off of South Africa.

Sea Stars

Most sea stars have five arms and look like stars. They are often called starfish, though they are not fish. There are about 1,800 species of sea stars. They come in many different colors. Most sea stars are 8 to 12 inches (20 to 30 centimeters) across.

Sea stars' arms are hollow and covered with spines. Many sea stars can grow another arm if they lose one. Sea stars move using hundreds of tube feet on their underside.

Sea stars' arms can be thick or thin. This blue sea star is sitting on top of another type of sea invertebrate, coral.

COMPARE AND CONTRAST

Sea stars use their tube feet to catch food and jellyfish use their tentacles. How do a sea star's tube feet and a jellyfish's tentacles work similarly? What is different about how they catch prey?

Many sea stars live in warm waters. The High Arctic sea star, however, lives in the cold waters of the Arctic Ocean.

In most sea stars, each tube foot has a suction cup on the end.

Most sea stars eat clams, oysters, and snails. They use their tube feet to pull apart the shells of larger prey. Some sea stars sweep food into their mouth. Others turn their stomach outward to take in their prey. Certain sea stars swallow prey whole.

SEA URCHINS

Sea urchins are part of a group of animals called **echinoderms**. Sea urchins look like globe-shaped pincushions. They are covered with long, movable spines that help the slow-moving animal "walk" and keep away enemies. Sea urchins live in all seas except those of the polar regions. They are found on the ocean floor, usually

The red sea urchin lives in the Pacific Ocean. This species often stays close to shore.

on hard surfaces. Sea urchins are usually red or purple. Some are less than an inch (2.5 centimeters) from side to side, while others measure 14

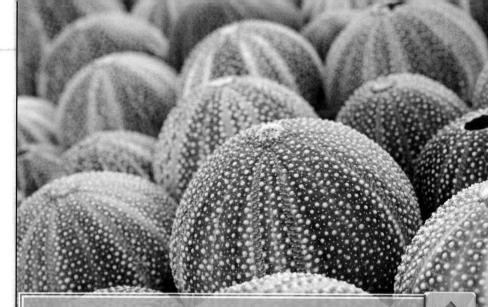

The sea urchin's test looks like a small ball. Some people eat the insides of sea urchins. In Japanese cuisine, the edible part of a sea urchin is called *uni*.

inches (36 centimeters) across. The spines of some sea urchins are up to 12 inches (30 centimeters) long.

Sea urchins have an internal skeleton called a test. Their spines stick out of the test and may be poisonous.

Sea urchins have tube feet, just like sea stars. The tube feet help the sea urchin grab food and bring it into its mouth. They feed mostly on plant material.

SPONGES

Sponges are unusual animals. They do not have the body parts that most animals have. They don't even move around. Instead sponges stay attached to a rock or coral reef. For a long time, people thought sponges were plants. Scientists discovered that sponges are animals after watching them eat food by drawing it into their bodies.

There are nearly 5,000 different species of sponge. Most live in the ocean, but some live in fresh water. Sponges come in a variety of shapes and sizes and colors.

◀◀

Sponges live all around the world. These red finger sponges live on a coral reef in Belize.

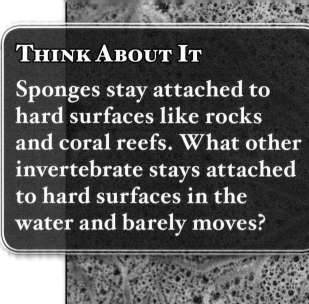

THINK ABOUT IT

Sponges stay attached to hard surfaces like rocks and coral reefs. What other invertebrate stays attached to hard surfaces in the water and barely moves?

In this close-up, you can see the tiny holes through which sponges draw in water.

They can be as small as a bean or as large as a person. Sponges can be smooth and mushy or hard and prickly.

A sponge's body is a soft mass of cells supported by a skeleton. Holes in a sponge's skin let water flow inside. Sponges get food and oxygen from the water.

CRABS

Crabs are members of a group of animals called crustaceans. There are about 4,500 species of crab. Crabs can be found in all oceans and in fresh water. Some crabs live on land, too. Crabs have a hard covering known as an exoskeleton. Crabs

The hard exoskeleton of a crab protects its soft insides. Crabs can also use the pinching claws on their first pair of legs to defend themselves.

VOCABULARY

Crustaceans are a group of animals that have exoskeletons and two pairs of antennas. Lobsters, shrimp, and crayfish are also crustaceans.

have five pairs of legs. The first pair has large pinching claws that help crabs eat and protect themselves. The tail of a crab is curled under its body.

Crabs come in a great range of sizes. Pea crabs may measure less than an inch (2.5 centimeters) across. The Japanese spider crab, on the other hand, may be more than 1 foot (30 centimeters) across and measure 12 feet (4 meters) from tip to tip of its outstretched legs.

The Japanese spider crab's leg span can reach up to 12 feet (4 meters) from claw to claw.

Most crabs eat dead or decaying material. Some crabs may feed on vegetable matter. Others eat small living animals. A crab's two large eyes extend from the head on movable stalks located above two pairs of antennas. The mouth is on the underside of the head.

All female crabs must lay their eggs in the water, even land crabs. The eggs are carried on the female's body until they hatch. Although some baby crabs leave the

THINK ABOUT IT

Crustaceans have a hard exoskeleton, but they are still invertebrates. Why do you think crustaceans like crabs are considered invertebrates?

◀◀

Crab larvae float at the surface of the water along with plankton, moving with water currents until they mature.

egg looking like small adults, most do not. Instead, a newly hatched crab is usually a tiny, see-through, legless creature that swims at the top of the water. At this stage the animal is called a zoea. Crabs then go through a process called metamorphosis. During this time they molt (shed their outside covering) many times. By the end of the process, the crab has developed into its adult form.

Ghost crabs' pale-colored bodies help them blend in with sand. Some crabs, like ghost crabs, have two different-sized front claws.

IMPORTANCE OF INVERTEBRATES

There are many types of sea invertebrates. They come in all shapes, colors, and sizes. Some have tentacles, while others have spines or claws. What they all have in common, besides a lack of a backbone, is that they are an important part of their ecosystems. Each animal in an ecosystem helps to keep the system in balance.

Pollution and global warming are threats to sea invertebrates. Polluted and warmer waters can cause

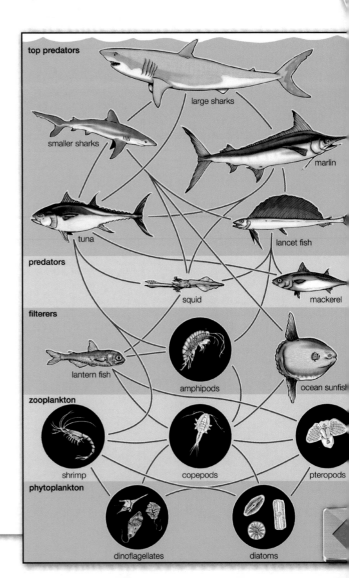

top predators

large sharks

smaller sharks

marlin

tuna

lancet fish

predators

squid

mackerel

filterers

lantern fish

amphipods

ocean sunfish

zooplankton

shrimp

copepods

pteropods

phytoplankton

dinoflagellates

diatoms

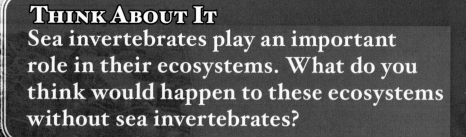

THINK ABOUT IT
Sea invertebrates play an important role in their ecosystems. What do you think would happen to these ecosystems without sea invertebrates?

A lot of garbage from humans ends up in the ocean. This garbage poses a threat to all forms of marine life.

organisms in the sea to die. It can also affect the food available to sea invertebrates, leaving them with nothing to eat.

Many people eat sea invertebrates, such as lobsters, crabs, and sea urchins. As a result, overfishing has become a serious problem. Some countries have put restrictions on fishing to prevent overfishing.

There are many groups working to conserve sea invertebrates and other sea animals. They work to increase awareness and change government policies. With their help, sea invertebrates will be around for many more years.

All animals are part of a food chain. Most animals are the prey of other animals as well as predators to other animals.

GLOSSARY

antennas Slender movable organs of sensation on the head of an arthropod (as an insect or a crab) that are made up of segments.

calcium carbonate A solid substance found in nature as limestone and marble and in plant ashes, bones, and shells and used especially in making lime and cement.

colonies Populations of plants or animals in a particular place that belong to one species.

ecosystem A system made up of a community of living things interacting with their environment especially under natural conditions.

global warming A warming of Earth's atmosphere and oceans that is predicted to result from the effects of air pollution.

metamorphosis The change in the form and habits of some animals from a young stage (as a tadpole or a caterpillar) to an adult stage (as a frog or a butterfly).

mollusks Members of a large group of invertebrate animals (such as snails, clams, and octopuses) with a soft body lacking segments and usually enclosed in a shell containing calcium.

overfishing To fish too much for a kind of fish or in a certain area.

paralyze To make something unable to act, function, or move.

pollution The action or process of making land, water, or air dirty and not safe or suitable to use.

species A category of living things that ranks below a genus, is made up of related individuals able to produce fertile offspring, and is identified by a two-part scientific name.

spine A stiff pointed, usually sharp, projecting part of a plant or animal.

tentacle A long flexible structure that sticks out usually around the head or mouth of an animal (as a jellyfish or sea anemone) and is used especially for feeling or grasping.

transparent Fine or sheer enough to be seen through.